8/03

Stink Bugs

and Other True Bugs

Concept and Product Development: Editorial Options, Inc.
Series Designer: Karen Donica
Book Author: Meish Goldish

For information on other World Book
products, visit us at our Web site at
http://www.worldbook.com

For information on sales to schools and libraries
in the United States, call 1-800-975-3250.

For information on sales to schools and libraries
in Canada, call 1-800-837-5365.

World Book, Inc.
233 N. Michigan Avenue
Chicago, IL 60601

Library of Congress Cataloging-in-Publication Data

Goldish, Meish
    Stink bugs and other true bugs / [book author, Meish Goldish].
       p. cm. -- (World Book's animals of the world)
    Summary: Questions and answers provide information about a variety of bugs,
    including the stink bug, harlequin bug, and giant water bug.
    ISBN 0-7166-1233-X -- ISBN 0-7166-1223-2 (set)
    1. Pentatomidae--Juvenile literature. 2. Hemiptera--Juvenile literature. [1.
Insects--Miscellanea. 2. Questions and answers.] I. World Book, Inc. II. Title. III. Series.
    QL523.P5 B74 2002
    595.7'54--dc21   2001046707

Printed in Malaysia

1 2 3 4 5 6 7 8 9 06 05 04 03 02

Picture Acknowledgments: Cover: © Stephen Collins, Photo Researchers; © Hermann Eisenbeiss, Photo Researchers; © David T. Roberts, Bruce Coleman Inc.; © K.G. Vock/Okapia from Photo Researchers; © Kent Wood, Photo Researchers.

© James H. Carmichael, Bruce Coleman Inc. 25; © Jack Clark, Animals Animals 11; © Stephen Collins, Photo Researchers 3, 7; © Stephen Dalton, Photo Researchers 31; © David Dennis, Animals Animals 49; © Alan & Linda Detrick, Photo Researchers 9; © Hermann Eisenbeiss, Photo Researchers 55; © P.S.U. Entomology from Photo Researchers 29; © Michael Fogden, Animals Animals 39; © Valerie Giles, Photo Researchers 35; © Bob Jensen, Bruce Coleman Inc. 5, 27; © Richard Kolar, Animals Animals 43; © George Lepp, Photo Researchers, 33; © Robert Lubeck, Animals Animals 51; © Joe & Carol McDonald, Tom Stack & Associates 9; © Gary Meszaros, Photo Researchers 4, 47, 57; © John Mitchell, Photo Researchers 53; © Stephen P. Parker, Photo Researchers 37; © Simon D. Pollard, Photo Researchers 9; © David T. Roberts, Photo Researchers 17; © James H. Robinson, Animals Animals 9, © Harry Rogers, Photo Researchers 15; © Kim Taylor, Bruce Coleman Inc. 21, 59; © K.G. Vock/Okapia from Photo Researchers 61; © Peter Ward, Bruce Coleman Inc. 19; © Larry West, Bruce Coleman Inc. 41; © Kent Wood, Photo Researchers 5, 45.

Illustrations: WORLD BOOK illustration by Michael DiGiorgio 13, 23; WORLD BOOK illustration by Kersti Mack 62.

World Book's Animals of the World

Stink Bugs
and Other True Bugs

How does my smell bug other animals?

World Book, Inc.
A Scott Fetzer Company
Chicago

Contents

How long does it take me to grow up?

Where can you see designs that look like me?

What do my bright colors tell predators?

What Is a True Bug?

The word *bug* is often used to describe any kind of insect or other little creature. However, not every "bug" is a true bug. In fact, scientists consider only an insect that belongs to the group called Hemiptera *(hih MIHP tuhr uh)* to be a true bug.

There are many species, or kinds, of true bugs. Stink bugs are true bugs. So are bed bugs, squash bugs, and water bugs. Some scientists also place insects such as cicadas *(suh KAY duhz)* and aphids *(AY fihdz)* into the same group as true bugs.

Like other insects, true bugs have six legs. But they don't have chewing mouthparts. Instead, true bugs suck their food through long, pointed beaks. Junebugs and ladybugs are insects. But since these types of insects have chewing mouthparts, they are not true bugs.

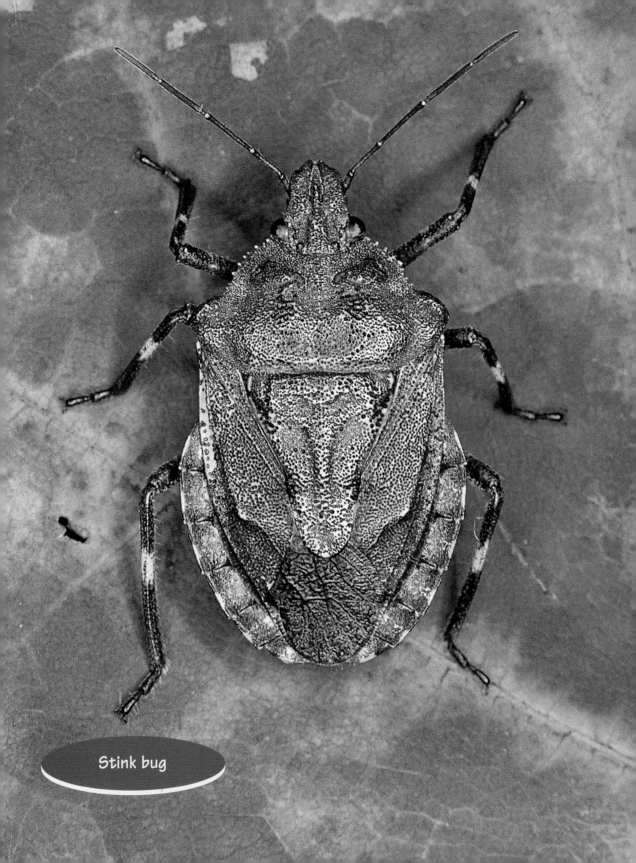

Stink bug

Where in the World Do True Bugs Live?

True bugs live all over the world. They are found everywhere, from hot jungles to cold polar regions. True bugs live in fields, gardens, orchards, woods, ponds, and streams.

Stink bugs make up a common family of true bugs. Like other true bugs, they make their homes in all climates around the world. Most species of stink bugs live in warm, tropical areas. But stink bugs live in colder places, too. Some species of stink bugs, for example, live in the cold northern regions of North America.

In spring and summer, you can find stink bugs on trees, bushes, grasses, weeds, flowers, and fruits.

Field

Woods

Garden

Pond

What Makes Stink Bugs True Bugs?

Like all true bugs, stink bugs have no chewing mouthparts. Instead, they have tubelike beaks called *rostrums* attached to their heads. The rostrum has four thin, sharp needles in it.

Many stink bugs sink their needles into plants. They use their needles to suck up the sap or juice that the plants use to transport and store food. Some stink bugs stick their beaks into other insects and suck their body fluids. When not feeding, stink bugs hold their beaks underneath their bodies between their front legs.

Like most true bugs, a stink bug has two pairs of wings. The back wings are so thin you can almost see through them. The front wings are thick and tough at the base and very thin at the tips. When a stink bug rests, the tips of its front wings cross, forming what looks like an "X."

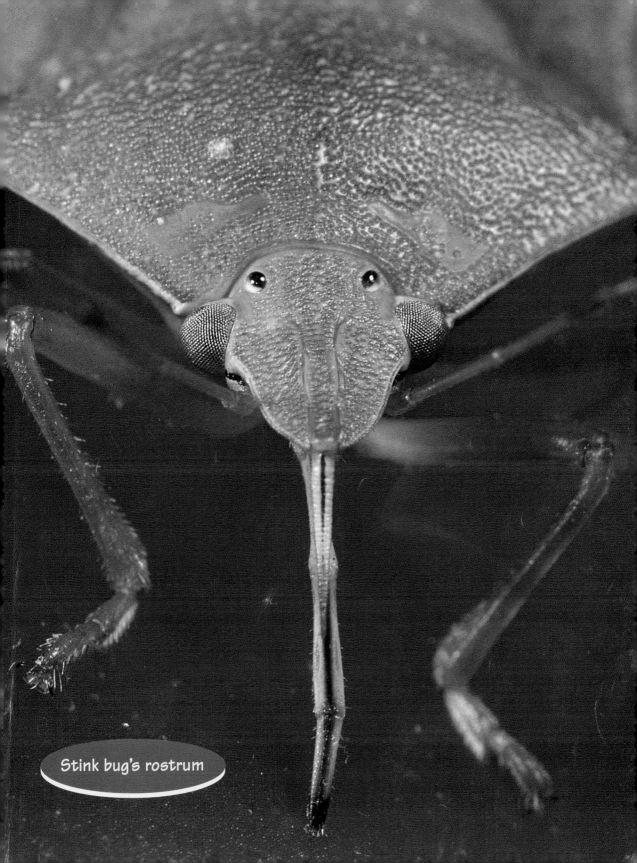

Stink bug's rostrum

How Is a Stink Bug Put Together?

A stink bug, like all insects, has a body that is divided into three sections. These sections are the head, the thorax *(THAWR aks),* and the abdomen. A tough shell, or exoskeleton *(EHK soh SKEHL uh tuhn),* protects the bug's entire body.

In addition to its rostrum, a stink bug has two large eyes on its head. These eyes are compound eyes. They are made up of many separate lenses. In between the eyes are two long feelers, or antennae *(an TEHN ee).* A stink bug uses its antennae to touch and to "pick up" scents.

A stink bug's middle section is the thorax. Its legs are attached to its thorax. If the stink bug has wings, they are also attached to the thorax.

The abdomen is a stink bug's hind section. Here is where you will find most of a stink bug's spiracles *(SPY ruh kuhlz),* or breathing holes. The bug's digestive and reproductive systems are also in its abdomen.

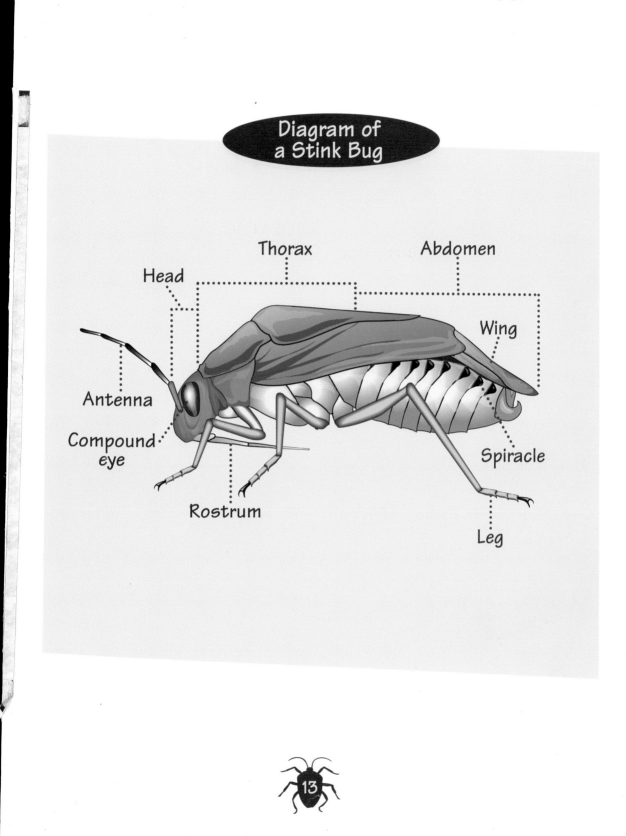

Diagram of a Stink Bug

Head

Thorax

Abdomen

Wing

Antenna

Compound eye

Spiracle

Rostrum

Leg

13

Why Are Some Stink Bugs Called Shield Bugs?

Many true bugs have hard, flat covers on their backs that look like shields. These covers are called *scutella (skyoo TEHL uh)*. They help protect, or shield, the bugs. That's why these bugs are also called shield bugs.

A scutellum is shaped like a triangle or a shield. On the bug in the picture, the scutellum is the triangle on its back. Some stink bugs and many related true bugs have scutella so big that they cover most of their backs.

Most stink bugs are from 1/4 to 3/4 of an inch (6 to 20 millimeters) long. Stink bugs come in a variety of colors. Some are all green. Some are all brown. Still others are black with white, yellow, orange, or red markings. Some stink bugs have bright colors. Others have dull colors.

Stink bug with scutellum

Does a Stink Bug Really Stink?

Phew! It sure does. A stink bug gives off a very bad smell if it is bothered. The smell comes from a stinky liquid that flows from two glands on the bug's thorax. Once released, the odor remains on whatever the stink bug touches.

To most predators, a stink bug tastes as bad as it smells. Many birds spit out stink bugs right after biting into them. However, other birds don't seem to mind a stink bug's taste.

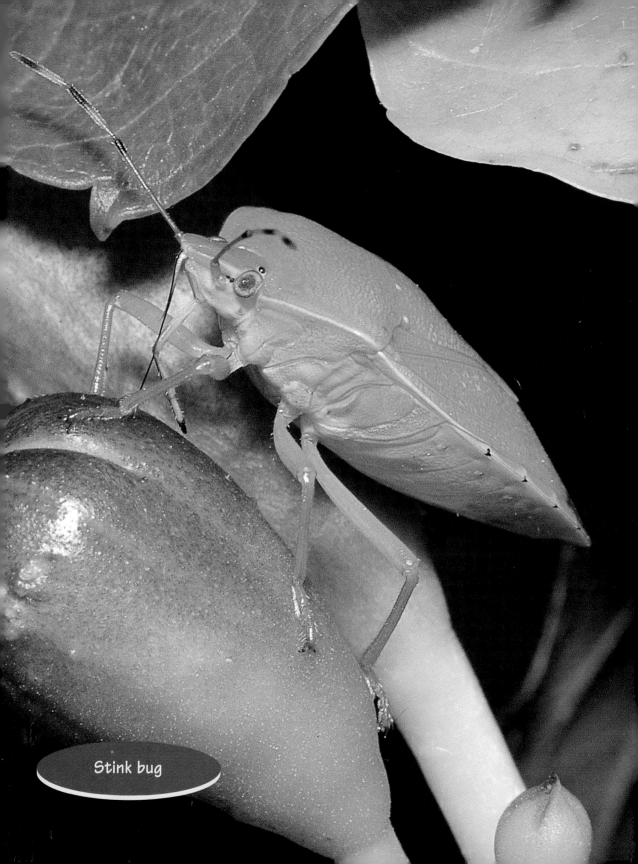

Stink bug

What Do Stink Bugs Feed On?

Most kinds of stink bugs suck the juices of plants. Some kinds suck the body fluids of insects. Others feed on both plants and insects.

Plant-sucking stink bugs feed on the juices of young fruits and seeds. Some also suck the sap from plants as well as the nectar from flowers. Green stink bugs, like the one you see here, often suck on crops like soybeans, rice, and tomatoes.

Some stink bugs can greatly damage a farmer's crops. But others can be helpful to farmers. The helpful stink bugs kill other insects that do more harm to plants than they do themselves. Such insects include certain types of beetles and caterpillars and even some other stink bugs.

Green stink bug
sucking juice

How Do Stink Bugs Find Mates?

Some stink bugs use special odors to attract mates. Smelling the odors helps partners find each other. Some kinds of stink bugs also attract mates with sound. They rub their legs or wings against their bodies to make noises similar to those of crickets. Mates are drawn to the sounds.

After mating, a female stink bug lays batches of eggs. Often she lays them in neat rows of 12 or 14 eggs each. The eggs are usually laid on plant leaves.

Stink bug eggs look like tiny barrels. The colors of the eggs depend on the type of stink bug that laid them. Green stink bugs, for example, lay yellow to green eggs that turn pink or gray.

In some species, a mother stink bug closely guards her nymphs *(NIHMFS),* or young, after they hatch. If the mother senses danger, she moves herself between the enemy and the nymphs. Then she acts as a shield and moves from side to side to protect the nymphs.

Stink bug with nymphs

How Do Stink Bugs Grow Up?

Stink bugs, like all true bugs, change as they grow. Like all insects, they go through a process called *metamorphosis (met uh MAWR fuh sihs).* But stink bugs don't change as much as many other insects do. Most insects go through four stages of development, while stink bugs go through three. That's why a stink bug's metamorphosis is incomplete.

As you can see in the diagram, a nymph has a shape much like an adult. Nymphs are smaller than adults, though. And nymphs don't have wings, as most adults do.

A nymph is born with a hard outer layer of skin that it soon outgrows. So the nymph molts, or sheds its skin. After the first molt, small padlike wings appear on the nymph's body. With each new molt, the wings grow longer. After the fifth and last molt, the wings are fully developed. A stink bug nymph becomes an adult after about a month.

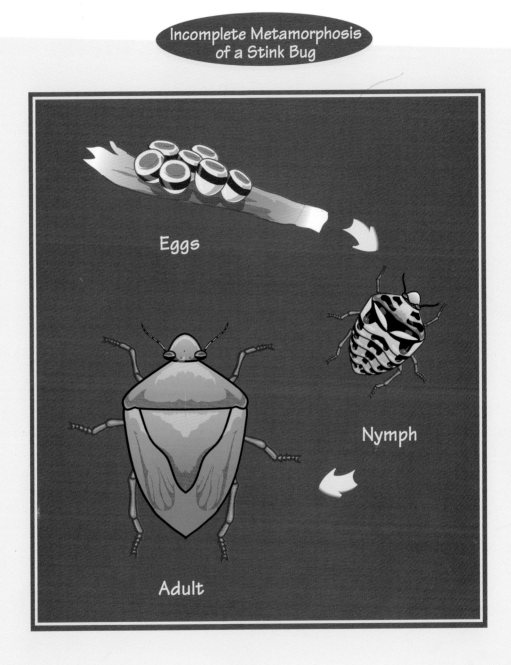

Eggs

Nymph

Adult

How Do Stink Bugs Defend Themselves?

A stink bug's main weapon of defense is its odor. When in danger, the stink bug releases a stinking liquid from its thorax. A bird or other predator often takes one whiff of the bug's rotten smell and leaves the tiny creature alone!

Some stink bugs also rely on their color for protection. Many blend in so well with their surroundings that they go unnoticed. Stink bugs that are green, for example, are hard to see on green leaves and stems. Other stink bugs, like the one you see here, have brown and gray patterns that help them blend in with tree bark.

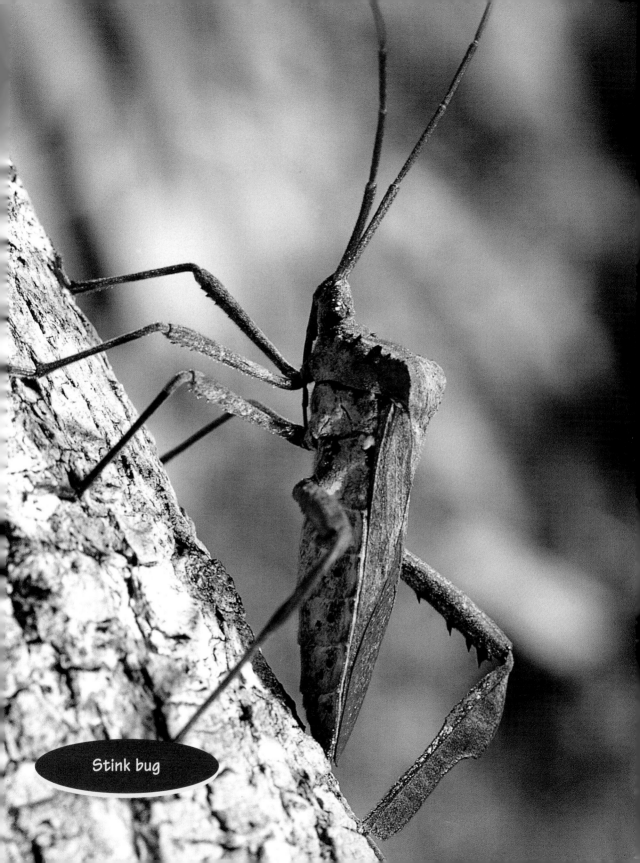

Stink bug

What Does a Harlequin Bug Look Like?

The harlequin *(HAHR luh kihn)* bug is a kind of stink bug. This stink bug is about 3/8 of an inch (10 millimeters) long. The harlequin bug may be small, but its colors make it easy to see. This bug's name means "many colors." The bug is black with bright red, orange, or yellow markings all over its body. Scientists think that these dazzling colors warn predators to stay away from this stinky bug.

Harlequin bugs often "hang out" on the leaves of their favorite crop: cabbage. These bugs often gather in large bunches. When they do, they can quickly destroy a cabbage crop.

Harlequin bugs once lived only in Mexico. Today, they live all over North America. All they need is a good cabbage crop to feed on!

Harlequin bug

What Bug Looks Like a Stink Bug, but Isn't?

A squash bug is a true bug that looks very much like a stink bug. The squash bug has a bad odor, too.

However, there is one easy way to tell these two bugs apart. They eat different plants. A squash bug feeds on crops that grow on vines. Its favorite food, as you might guess, is squash. It also loves pumpkins. Squash bugs suck the juice from the leaves and stems of these plants. So if you see a true bug on a pumpkin or a squash, it is probably a squash bug.

A squash bug nymph is born with a red head and legs. As it grows, the bug turns black or gray. An adult squash bug is 5/8 of an inch (16 millimeters) long.

A main predator of the squash bug is the tachinid *(TAK uh nihd)* fly. This tiny fly lands on the back of a squash bug. Once there, the fly lays an egg. Soon the baby fly hatches and tunnels into the squash bug. The tachinid fly eats the bug's insides. The squash bug may die as a result.

Squash bugs on
a pumpkin

How Did Bed Bugs Get Their Name?

Bed bugs were so named because they were often found in people's beds. That brought about the saying, "Goodnight, sleep tight, don't let the bed bugs bite." Today, people keep things cleaner than they used to. Fewer bed bugs live in people's beds. However, bed bugs are still common in some homes.

Like some kinds of true bugs, bed bugs can be serious pests. But these bugs don't destroy crops. Instead, they feed only on blood. They bite humans, dogs, cats, birds, and many other warm-blooded animals. Bed bugs use their sharp beaks to pierce the skin of their victims. Then they suck out blood.

The bed bug is one of the few true bugs that has no wings. The reddish-brown bug is about 1/4 of an inch (6 millimeters) long. During the day, this tiny bug can hide almost anywhere—in cracks in furniture, floors, or wall plaster. It can also hide in a rug, under a mattress, or behind peeling wallpaper. At night, a bed bug makes its way to a victim to feed.

Bed bug on skin

31

Which True Bugs Love Corn?

Chinch bugs love to suck the fluids of corn plants. These true bugs also feed on other grain plants, such as barley, rye, and wheat. That's what makes these bugs pests to farmers.

Chinch bugs are very tiny. They are only about 1/6 of an inch (4 millimeters) long. They spend the winter in dry grass and weeds. In the spring, the bugs lay eggs. They feed in fields of grain.

When grain stops growing and begins to ripen, the juices inside the plants dry up. So, chinch bugs must find new sources of food. Often they move to newly planted corn fields. Since the corn plants are still growing, there is plenty of juice to feed on.

Chinch bug

What Do Boxelder Bugs Feed On?

Boxelder bugs live in boxelder trees in the eastern and midwestern United States. The bugs suck the leaves, flowers, and seeds of the trees they are named after. They also suck on maple and ash trees. However, boxelder bugs do little damage to any trees.

You can recognize a boxelder bug by its red and black colors. This bug is about 1/2 inch (13 millimeters) long. In the summer, large numbers of boxelder bugs cover the trunks of boxelder trees.

Most boxelder bugs don't stay on trees all year long. In the fall, they look for warm places to spend the winter. They may settle on the sunny sides of fences, rocks, and buildings. In the spring, the bugs leave their winter homes and return to the trees to feed.

Boxelder bugs

How Sneaky Are Ambush Bugs?

Ambush bugs are very sneaky. Many kinds of these true bugs hide in flowers and wait for spiders or insects to come along. Ambush bugs use their strong front legs to grab their surprised prey. Then they quickly sink their sharp beaks into their victims and suck the fluids.

Ambush bugs are 3/8 to 1/2 inch (10 to 13 millimeters) long. Some kinds have yellow bodies that help them hide on flowers of the same color. Flies or other prey that visit flowers don't notice the ambush bugs until it is too late.

Ambush bugs have powerful legs that are hooked at the ends. These bugs use their legs to catch and hold onto their victims. The victims may be bigger than the ambush bugs are themselves. In fact, ambush bugs often prey on insects as big as bumblebees and wasps!

Ambush bug with prey

How Do Assassin Bugs Kill?

Assassin bugs use their sharp beaks to stab their prey. Like many other predatory true bugs, assassin bugs shoot poison into the bodies of their victims. The poison causes the prey to become paralyzed *(PAIR uh lyzd)*, or unable to move. The poison also makes the prey's insides soft and soggy. The assassin bugs can then suck up all the juices of their prey. All that's left of the victims are empty shells!

Assassin bugs grow as long as 1 3/5 inches (4 centimeters). Many kinds have thin bodies that look weak but are really strong. Assassin bugs can kill most insects they go after. The front legs of assassin bugs have special sticky hairs. These hairs help the bugs hold onto their victims while stabbing the victims with their beaks.

Like ambush bugs, assassin bugs wait in or near flowers for their victims. The bugs often hide out in goldenrods, asters, and other members of the daisy family.

Assassin bug stabbing prey

Do Toad Bugs Hop?

Yes, toad bugs do hop—just as toads do! Toad bugs live along the muddy banks of ponds, lakes, and streams. There, they feed on tiny water insects. Toad bugs often capture their prey by hopping up in the air and landing on them.

Toad bugs don't just act like toads. These bugs look like toads, too. Toad bugs have short, wide bodies that are usually brown. Their bodies often appear to be covered in "warts." And they have large heads with eyes that are set wide apart— much as toads do. So how can you tell toad bugs apart from toads? Toad bugs have six legs while toads have just four.

Toad bug

Which True Bugs Are Really Flat?

Flat bugs are about as flat as thin pieces of bark. And bark is just what these true bugs look like. Flat bugs spend much of their time on the sides of trees. Most flat bugs are dark brown. Their brown coloring helps them blend in with the bark around them.

Flat bugs are flat enough to crawl into tiny cracks of old, rotting trees. They also crawl under tree bark. Flat bugs hide in the small spaces and suck on fungus growing there. Because they like fungus so much, flat bugs are sometimes called fungus bugs.

Flat bug

Which True Bugs Look Like Lace?

Lace bugs look like small pieces of white or gray lace. Many kinds of lace bugs live on trees, such as sycamore, ash, hickory, mulberry, and oak.

Lace bugs gather in groups and feed on the bottoms of tree leaves. A gathering of lace bugs can make a leaf look as if it has white spots. At first, the white spots are the bodies of the lace bugs. But then, as the bugs suck out the sap, other white spots appear, too. Sucking lace bugs can do real damage to a tree.

A lace bug is tiny—only 1/8 inch (3 millimeters) long. The female lays her eggs in slits made on the tree leaves. She then covers her eggs with a thin, sticky liquid that hardens into tiny cones. The cones protect the eggs until they hatch. The female may lay 100 or more eggs on a single leaf!

Lace bug

Which True Bugs Walk on Pond Bottoms?

Water scorpions walk very slowly on pond bottoms. These bugs have thin bodies that are about 2 inches (5 centimeters) long. Many kinds of water scorpions look very much like small sticks. They don't swim very well. But these bugs can fly. If their pond dries up, water scorpions can fly for miles to find a new home.

A water scorpion eats insects, tadpoles, small fish, and salamanders. The bug grabs its prey with its strong front legs. Then the water scorpion uses its beak to stab its victim and to suck out the victim's body fluids. Because a water scorpion looks like a stick, its victim may not even see it coming.

A water scorpion doesn't have gills to breathe oxygen from water, as a fish does. Instead, it has a breathing tube on its abdomen. The bug uses its tube like a straw to suck in the air. To do this, the bug climbs up a water plant and lifts its breathing tube above the water.

Water scorpion

Which True Bug Swims on Its Back?

A backswimmer does! This bug paddles across the water, using its back legs like the oars of a boat. Like a water scorpion, a backswimmer can also fly.

A backswimmer can stay underwater for several hours at a time. Usually, it rests just below the surface. But sooner or later, it needs air.

A backswimmer has tiny hairlike growths on its body. It pushes these out so they are above the surface of water. This causes air to flow beneath the surface. The backswimmer traps the air in a bubble under its wings. The bug then breathes in the air through its breathing holes.

A backswimmer's enemies include fish and birds. But this true bug's colors help it hide from predators. The backswimmer's back is light-colored, like the sky. And its belly is dark, like the bottom of a pond. So predators often can't see a backswimmer from below or above.

Backswimmer

49

Do Water Boatmen Live on Boats?

Water boatmen don't live on boats. However, like backswimmers, they are very comfortable in the water. In fact, water boatmen carry their own air supply with them as they swim. They keep the air under their wings and all around their bodies.

Unlike other true bugs, a water boatman has a soft beak. The bug cannot use its beak to stab its food. Instead, a water boatman uses its short front legs to collect algae *(AL jee)* and the remains of dead animals and water plants. The bug then sucks on what it has gathered.

A water boatman uses its middle and back legs for swimming. The bug can also fly out of water. Like many true bugs that live in the water, it is often attracted by lights that are near a lake or pond.

Water boatman

How Big Are Giant Water Bugs?

Giant water bugs live up to their name. Species that live in the tropics can grow up to 4 inches (10 centimeters) long. Giant water bugs are the largest of all true bugs!

Like other water bugs, giant water bugs live in freshwater ponds, streams, and lakes. These bugs are very strong swimmers, but they spend most of their time sitting and waiting for prey. They catch insects, tadpoles, salamanders, frogs, and fish. The giant water bug you see here is catching an animal that is larger than itself—a frog. The bug grabs the frog with its front legs. The legs hook tightly onto the victim. Then the water bug stabs the frog with its rostrum and sucks out its insides.

Giant water bugs take care of their eggs in an unusual way. The female produces a sticky liquid on the male's back. Then she lays 100 or more eggs in the liquid. Enemies stay away from the eggs, since the male is right there to protect them!

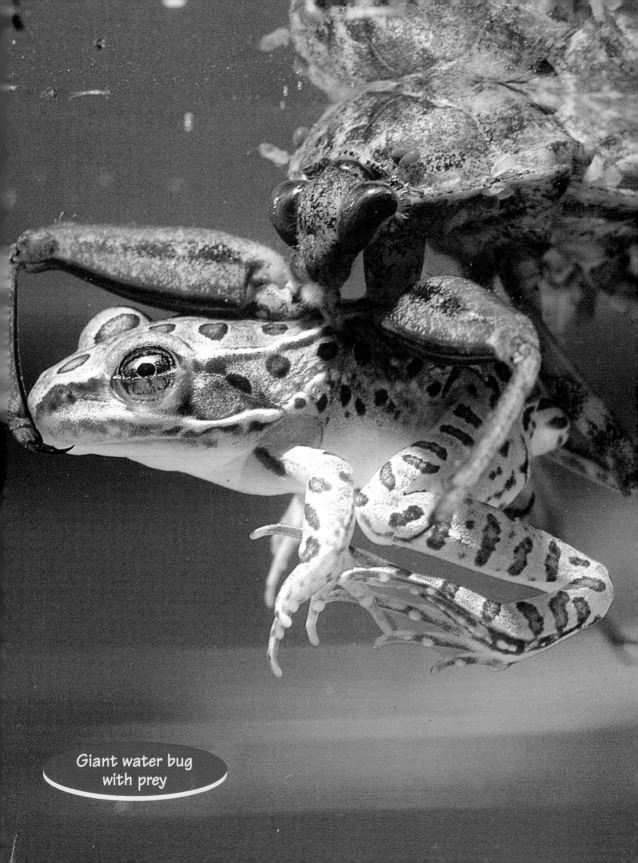

Giant water bug
with prey

Which Water Bugs Skate?

Water striders can move quickly along the water's surface. These true bugs look as if they are "skating" on water. They don't sink because of the way they spread out their long, thin back legs. Their weight is spread over a large area, so these bugs can actually slide along the surface of water.

Water striders are about 3/4 inch (19 millimeters) long. Many live on freshwater ponds and streams. These bugs use waves to find food. When insects fall in the water, they make tiny ripples. Water striders feel the ripples with their feet. They skate to the source and stab their victims with their beaks!

Some species of water striders live on the ocean. In fact, they are the only insects that can live their entire lives on the ocean. These bugs skate around and feed on dead fish and other animals they find.

Water strider

What Are Almost True Bugs?

Many scientists classify cicadas, aphids, and leafhoppers with the true bugs in the group Hemiptera. Other scientists place them in a separate group called Homoptera *(huh MOP tuhr uh).* Either way, scientists agree that cicadas and other "almost true bugs" are closely related to true bugs. Both groups use similar sucking mouthparts to feed.

Cicadas are 1 to 2 inches (2.5 to 5 centimeters) long and have even longer wings. Their wings lie over their bodies like raised roofs. You can tell cicadas from true bugs by taking a close look at their wings. The front wings of cicadas lack the thick, tough bases that true bug wings have.

Cicadas have some of the most interesting life cycles among insects. Many cicada nymphs remain in the ground 4 to 7 years before they become adults. Others take 13 to 17 years to develop! However, after spending all that time growing, adult cicadas live for only a few weeks out of the ground.

Cicadas

How Do Leafhoppers Get Around?

Leafhoppers travel in several ways. As their name suggests, leafhoppers can hop from leaf to leaf when on plants. They also fly. And some leafhoppers also get around by running sideways!

Most leafhoppers are only 1/20 to 1/4 inch (1.3 to 6.4 millimeters) long. Some leafhoppers are brightly colored. Others are dull green or brown.

Leafhoppers live in grassy meadows and gardens throughout the world. They suck on the juices of plants. As a result, the plants often wilt. Many leafhoppers also carry disease.

Leafhopper

Are True Bugs in Danger?

Most true bugs are quite tiny, so they are always in danger of being eaten by birds, spiders, and other insects. Humans are also an enemy of many true bugs.

Farmers may use chemicals to kill true bugs that harm their crops. Gardeners may do the same. Some people also release insects that are harmful to true bugs and their relatives. Ladybugs, which eat aphids, are sometimes released to protect crops that aphids feed on.

Some true bugs that live in tropical places may become extinct. As tropical rain forests are cut down, species living in them lose their homes. Scientists believe that many unknown species of true bugs and other insects live in these forests. They may die out before they are even discovered. But most true bugs are so numerous that they are not in danger of disappearing.

Stink bug

True Bug Fun Facts

→ True bugs (and all other insects) have no eyelids.

→ Bed bugs can go over a year without a meal.

→ Giant water bugs are also known as electric-light bugs because they are attracted to lights at night.

→ Bed bugs may crawl from house to house.

→ Some assassin bugs are also called kissing bugs because they stab their beaks into the faces of sleeping people.

→ There are more than 5,000 different kinds of stink bugs.

→ Some assassin bugs can make hissing sounds by scraping their rostrums against the undersides of their bodies.

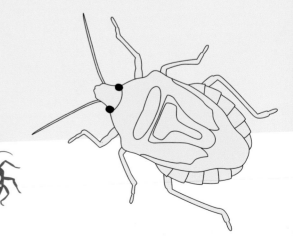

Glossary

abdomen The back part of an insect's body.

algae Simple plantlike organisms.

antennae The feelers on an insect's head.

aphid A small insect that sucks sap from plants.

compound eye An eye made up of many separate lenses.

digestive system A group of organs that break food down into smaller parts that the body can use.

exoskeleton A tough shell that protects an insect's body.

extinct No longer existing.

fungus A plantlike organism that cannot make its own food.

incomplete metamorphosis A true bug's growth process from egg to nymph to adult.

metamorphosis Going through extreme changes between birth and adult phases of life.

molt To shed the outer shell and grow a new one.

nectar A sugary liquid that flowering plants produce.

nymph An insect that is in the developmental stage between egg and adult.

paralyzed Unable to feel or to move.

parasite An animal that lives on or in another animal and feeds on it.

predator An animal that preys on another for food.

rostrum A tubelike beak on a true bug's head.

scutellum A hard, protective cover on the backs of some true bugs.

spiracle An insect's breathing holes.

thorax The middle part of an insect's body, between the head and abdomen.

Index

(**Boldface** indicates a photo or illustration.)

For more information about true bugs, try these resources:

Big Book of Bugs, by Theresa Greenaway, Dorling Kindersley, 2000.

Eyewitness: Insects, by Lawrence Mound, Dorling Kindersley, 2000.

True Bugs: When Is a Bug Really a Bug?, by Sara Swan Miller, Franklin Watts, 1998.

http://la.lti.cs.cmu.edu/callan/k12/ScavHunt2/insects/WW565.htm.

http://www.enchantedlearning.com/subjects/insects/bugs/Harlequinbug.shtml.

http://www.uwex.edu/ces/cty/milwaukee/urbanag/bugnet/intfloor/leaffoot/leaffoot.html.

Hemiptera Classification

Scientists classify animals by placing them into groups. The animal kingdom is a group that contains all the world's animals. Phylum, class, order, and family are smaller groups. Each phylum contains many classes. A class contains orders, an order contains families, and a family contains individual species. Each species also has its own scientific name. Here is how the animals in this book fit in to this system.

Insects and their relatives (Phylum Arthropoda)

Insects (Class Insecta)

True bugs and "almost true bugs" (Order Hemiptera)

Ambush bugs (Family Phymatidae)

Aphids (Family Aphididae)*

Assassin bugs (Family Reduviidae)

Backswimmers (Family Notonectidae)

Bed bug and its relatives (Family Cimicidae)
Bed bug . . . . *Cimex lectularius*

Boxelder bug and its relatives (Family Rhopalidae)
Boxelder bug . . . . *Leptocoris trivittatus*

Chinch bug and its relatives (Family Lygaeidae)

Cicadas (Family Cicadidae)*

Flat bugs (Family Aradidae)

Giant water bugs (Family Belostomatidae)

Lace bugs (Family Tingidae)

Leafhoppers (Family Cicadellidae)*

Squash bug and its relatives (Family Coreidae)
Squash bug . . . . *Anasa tristis*

Stink bugs (Family Pentatomidae)
Green stink bug . . . . *Acrosternum hilare*
Harlequin bug . . . . *Murgantia histrionica*

Toad bugs (Family Gelastocoridae)

Water boatmen (Family Corixidae)

Water scorpions (Family Nepidae)

Water striders (Family Gerrudae)

*Not all scientists include aphids, cicadas, and leafhoppers in the order Hemiptera. Some scientists place these insects and their relatives into a separate order, Homoptera.